ideals®
CHRISTMAS

2003

Dedicated to a celebration—through poetry and prose—of the American ideals of faith in God, loyalty to country, and love of family.

It is Christmas in the heart that puts Christmas in the air. —W. T. Ellis

IDEALS—Vol. 60, No. 6 November 2003 IDEALS (ISSN 0019-137X, USPS 256-240) is published six times a year: January, March, May, July, September, and November by IDEALS PUBLICATIONS, a division of Guideposts, 39 Seminary Hill Road, Carmel, NY 10512. Copyright © 2003 by IDEALS PUBLICATIONS, a division of Guideposts. All rights reserved. The cover and entire contents of IDEALS are fully protected by copyright and must not be reproduced in any manner whatsoever. Title IDEALS registered U.S. Patent Office. Printed and bound in USA by Quebecor Printing. Printed on Weyerhaeuser Husky. The paper used in this publication meets the minimum requirements of American National Standard for Information Sciences—Permanence of Paper for Printed Library Materials, ANSI Z39.48-1984. Periodicals postage paid at Carmel, New York, and additional mailing offices. POSTMASTER: Send address changes to Ideals, 39 Seminary Hill Road, Carmel, NY 10512. For subscription or customer service questions, contact Ideals Publications, a division of Guideposts, 39 Seminary Hill Road, Carmel, NY 10512. Fax 845-228-2115. Reader Preference Service: We occasionally make our mailing lists available to other companies whose products or services might interest you. If you prefer not to be included, please write to Ideals Customer Service.

ISBN 0-8249-1210-1   GST 893989236

Visit the *Ideals* website at www.idealsbooks.com

Cover: Schoolchildren prepare for the Christmas holidays in Linda Nelson Stocks' original painting HOLLY HILL SCHOOL.

Inside front cover: Artist Shelly Reeves Smith captures a moment of winter quiet in JUST RESTING. *© 2003 Shelly Reeves Smith. Courtesy of Main Street Press, Ltd.*

Inside back cover: The neighborhood children have parked their sleds and headed indoors after a day of winter fun in A WARM KITCHEN *by Artist Ned Young. © 2003 Ned Young. Courtesy of Bookmark, Ltd.*

In This Issue

QUIETLY WINTER

Micheline Hull Dolan

Winter sneaked in;
I was caught unaware.
One day I awoke
And the leaves weren't there.

The pumpkins, bright orange,
Had long since been pies,
And the clear azure hue
Was gone from the skies.

That cool nippy chill
Became suddenly cold,
And the breeze, oh so gentle,
Was a wind, downright bold.

For Winter had tiptoed,
Nodded her head,
And a blanket of white
Put autumn to bed.

WHEN WINTER COMES

Nora M. Bozeman

When Winter comes and cloaks the land,
She holds snow crystals in her hand.
She fashions trees in fleecy white
And icicles the eaves at night.

When Winter comes and snowflakes fly
Like dancing diamonds from the sky,
She coats my windowpane in lace
Where old Jack Frost has kissed her face.

When Winter comes and north winds blow,
They drift the mounds of sculptured snow;
And I asleep in ermine arms
Dream of Winter's wondrous charms.

Snow clings to the red footbridge of Kubota Gardens in Seattle, Washington. Photo by Terry Donnelly.

First Snowfall

Kay Hoffman

All through the night the snowflakes fell
Without the slightest sound
To make a winter wonderland
Of our little town.

The fir trees wore a regal look
In sequined bridal dress;
The lamppost donned a white top hat,
His elegance expressed.

Each little home a picture
Knee-deep in drifts of snow;
A postcard only God could send
To set our hearts aglow.

A stillness fills the morning air,
No sounds to bring alarm
But just a sleepy little town
Cradled in winter's arms.

Summer lauds her fairest rose,
Autumn flaunts her brightest shawl,
But there's nothing quite so lovely
As winter's first snowfall.

A snowman surveys this Boston, Massachusetts, neighborhood after a snowstorm. Photos by Dianne Dietrich Leis.

Overleaf: Twilight descends on the icy waters of Flat Creek in the National Elk Refuge of Jackson Hole, Wyoming. Photo by Terry Donnelly.

Silver Morn

Dorothy P. Albaugh

This is a silver day. Each blade
Of grass is silver filigree.
It outlines shingles on the roof
And every black-twigged winter tree.

Against the gray blue sky above
There is a singing silver dove.
Awake! A day of such great cost
Is far too precious to be lost!

Transformation

Marilyn Kratz

The winter world of yesterday
Was cold and bleak and brown,
Then overnight a snowstorm came
And magic touched the town.

The evergreens wear cozy capes
That glisten ermine white;
The lawn's new carpet has the look
Of sugar, clean and bright.

Each post along the backyard fence
Has donned a pointed hat;
And power lines, once long and thin,
Look furry now, and fat.

Ice-laden branches glisten throughout a forest near Warren, Vermont.
Photo by William H. Johnson.

FIRST DEEP SNOW OF WINTER

The first deep snow of winter fills me with awe and wonder, especially if it comes at Christmastime. I want to be out of doors, letting the snowflakes sweep down around me, clinging to my eyebrows and eyelashes, to the cold tip of my nose, to my cap and mittens and overcoat. I want to be outside with the flakes as they fall to the ground, submerging the frosted grass and the frozen fields, the furrows, and the bare boughs of trees.

I want to feel the snowstorm, feel the sting of its wind against my face, the icy cold caresses from the heavy, leaden skies. I want to watch the storm as it piles the snow deeper and deeper over grass and walls, building hedges into mounds of white, transforming roofs into slopes of loveliness. I want to watch the storm transform the countryside into a feathery fluffiness.

I like to watch the snowstorm even as it continues into the night. The snowflakes glitter like diamonds in the radiance of light pouring out of the windows of my house. I am witness to a miracle that transforms the hills from a dull brown landscape into one of beauty and cleanliness.

I think how restless the hills must have been before the snow, heaving in the change between each night's freeze and the warmth of the daytime sun, the miniature castles of crystal pushed up from the ground by frost, settling back again when the sun is high.

Like a restless child at bedtime, the land has tried in vain to resist the urgency to sleep. But the first deep snow brings that blissful rest, as Nature, with hands as loving as a mother's hands, tucks in the blankets around the neck and shoulders of the hills, building within a warmth conducive to a winter of rest.

The author of three books, Lansing Christman has contributed to Ideals *for almost thirty years. Mr. Christman has also been published in several American, international, and braille anthologies. He lives in rural South Carolina.*

The red gambrel barn of a Sanbornton, New Hampshire, farm nestles under a blanket of fresh snow. Photo by William H. Johnson.

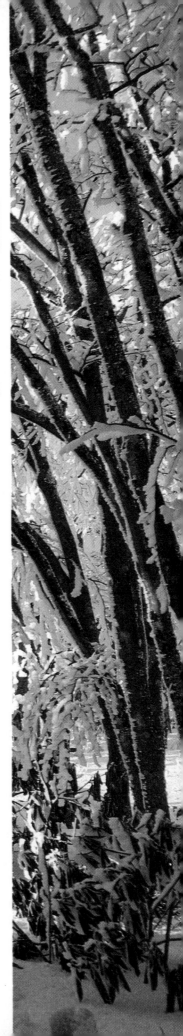

The Homey Road

Agnes Davenport Bond

There is a homey road
That leads to lighted windows
Where the candles glow,
Where wreaths of holly blend
With evergreen and mistletoe.

There is a homey road
That leads across the mountains
And the seven seas,
A homey road that leads
To open fires and Christmas trees.

There is a homey road
That ends at joyous meetings
And dear familiar sights,
Where love and happiness
Are linked with peaceful candle lights.

*A tree-lined lane beckons on Beech Mountain of the
Blue Ridge Mountains in North Carolina. Photo by Norman Poole.*

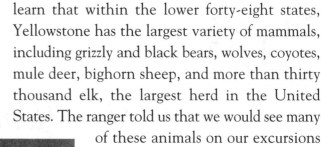

TRAVELER'S DIARY

D. Fran Morley

YELLOWSTONE NATIONAL PARK

Last winter, a new world opened up for me in the snow-covered majesty of Yellowstone National Park. I learned to appreciate the grand beauty that winter brings to this magnificent landscape that has been attracting visitors for more than 130 years.

The park includes natural wonders of such an astounding magnitude that early descriptions of them were dismissed as fabrications before an official exploration provided photographic proof in 1871. A year later, President Ulysses S. Grant signed the park into existence, setting aside 2.2 million acres of wilderness—nearly the size of Connecticut—expressly for "the benefit and enjoyment of the people." This was, of course, long before most people could easily travel to this mountainous region.

A frost-covered bison grazes in the Upper Geyser Basin of Yellowstone National Park, Wyoming. Photo by Terry Donnelly.

Today, traveling to Yellowstone is easy; my husband and I flew into Bozeman, Montana, and then drove a rental car to the park's north entrance at Gardiner, the only entrance that is open to automobiles in the winter. The sun was disappearing behind the mountains as we arrived at Mammoth Hot Springs Lodge, an impressive structure built in 1937 that combines traditional western style with tasteful art deco touches.

That evening, with steaming cups of cocoa in hand, we joined others in the library as a ranger described the park's wildlife. I was impressed to learn that within the lower forty-eight states, Yellowstone has the largest variety of mammals, including grizzly and black bears, wolves, coyotes, mule deer, bighorn sheep, and more than thirty thousand elk, the largest herd in the United States. The ranger told us that we would see many of these animals on our excursions into the park, except for the bears, which had been tucked into their dens since November and would not emerge until March.

The next morning we boarded a bus for a tour along the one road that is open during the winter. Overnight a few inches of fresh powder had been added to the knee-deep accumulation of snow, which made conditions perfect for those who chose to rent snowmobiles for a guided tour. Visitors can also rent cross-country skis, snowshoes, and even appropriate cold-weather clothing.

The ranger explained that in the winter, grazing animals descend from the higher elevations in search of food, and we wouldn't have to wait long to see them. Soon after leaving the lodge, we halted to watch several large elk graze nearby. Cameras clicked madly as we all enjoyed our close encounter with some of Yellowstone's wild animals.

As we continued on through the park, we were awestruck by the snow-capped vistas that faced us with each turn. The harsh reality of life in the wilderness became evident, too, as we watched several wolves chase a herd of elk that spun and turned in unison, churning up the snow in their attempt to escape. The wolves, we learned, were reintroduced to the park in 1995. Officials rarely, if ever, interfere with park animals' behavior, as we observed.

As the wide Lamar Valley opened before us, we were thrilled to see several dozen bison grazing peacefully just off the road as two coyotes lounged on a nearby rise. Had the bison been on the road, we would have had to wait for them to move. Animals always have the right of way in Yellowstone!

Back at the lodge, we took a snowshoe trek around the hot springs, being careful to stay on the trails. Two-thirds of the world's hot springs and geysers are in Yellowstone; the Earth's molten rock layer, or magma, lies only about two miles below the surface here, compared with six miles or more in most other places. The contrast between the cold mountain air and the steaming springs created huge clouds of vapor that billowed and puffed around the bubbling springs. The sunlight sparkled through the ice on nearby trees, sending rainbows through the mist.

The next day we traveled via snowcoach—a kind of van on tractor treads—to the park's most famous geyser, Old Faithful. Right on schedule, super-heated water burst forth, rising nearly two hundred feet into the air. In the summer, hundreds of people fill the viewing area, but on this pristine winter day, we were nearly alone.

Morning light highlights the steam venting from Castle Geyser in Yellowstone National Park. Photo by Terry Donnelly.

Later, at the Albright Visitor's Center and Museum at Mammoth Hot Springs, we learned that more than three million visitors from all over the world come to Yellowstone every year. Most crowd into the park during June and July, when traffic jams can rival those in any city. During the off-season, visitors have to be more flexible because brutal winter weather can often interfere with travel plans, but winter also gives visitors a unique opportunity to explore one of our country's grandest areas. We were sorry that we couldn't see more of Yellowstone—winter makes much of it inaccessible to all but the hardiest traveler—but the season provided a peace and solitude like the earliest explorers might have experienced when they first ventured into the land now called Yellowstone.

When not gallivanting around the country, travel writer Fran Morley spends time with her husband and their cat, Gracie, in beautiful Fairhope, Alabama.

Winter Farmhouses

Hellen Gay Miller

Farmhouses seem to nestle down
Closer to earth than homes in town.
Their walls are wide, their eaves are low,
Their roofs reach down to meet the snow,
And some wear mufflers, thick and warm,
Of brown leaves banked against the storm.
Others, with ells spread out like wings,
And long, long tails of sheds and things,

Are parked like airplanes at ease
In hangars of snug maple trees.

This one is mothered by a hill,
In whose warm lap the winds grow still,
While that one, tucked where cedars tall
Protect it with a windward wall,
Is overarched by one great tree—
An elm as old as memory.

Where miles are long and cold and dark,
These homesteads hold the only spark
Of life, so little homes on farms
Must nestle closest in earth's arms.

*Fresh snowfall covers a farm building in Capitol Reef
National Park, Utah. Photo by Terry Donnelly.*

LEGENDARY AMERICANS

Peggy Schaefer

ROBERT E. PEARY

In his many years of exploring the Arctic, Robert E. Peary endured bitter cold, endless ice, inadequate supplies, and the loss of men and dogs along the way. But his enthusiasm and his determination to be the first person to reach the North Pole paid off richly when he arrived at the Pole with his trusted assistant, Matthew Henson, and four Eskimo companions on April 6, 1909. Upon his ship's return to Indian Harbor in Labrador, Peary telegraphed the news services: "Stars and Stripes nailed to the Pole."

Family Years

Robert Edwin Peary was born in Cresson, Pennsylvania, in 1856. His father died when young "Bertie," as Peary was called, was three years old, whereupon he and his mother moved to Maine to be near her family. Always a good student, Bert studied engineering at Bowdoin College on a scholarship. In 1877, eager to explore the world, he joined the U.S. Navy Corps of Engineers.

Early Expeditions

The Navy sent Peary to Nicaragua to study the feasibility of building a canal. After plans for the canal stalled, Peary returned to Washington, D. C. There his interest in the Arctic grew as he immersed himself in reading accounts of northern exploration.

Peary began to prepare for a trip not yet even planned. He studied ice currents in the north, explored the use of sledges and dogs to haul provisions, and developed a plan for building shelters. Peary also studied how the Eskimos used furs, food, and igloos.

In 1886, Peary took a six-month leave from the Navy to indulge his dream of Arctic exploration. After arriving in Greenland, he met up with Christian Maigaard. The two men struggled across nearly a hundred miles of ice and snow before turning around and heading home. The experience only whetted Peary's appetite for exploration.

Peary returned to Greenland in 1891 and 1893. Matthew Henson, whom Peary had hired as his assistant for his Navy assignment in Nicaragua, accompanied Peary on these journeys, as did Peary's wife, Josephine. Henson earned fame as the first African-American to explore the Arctic.

During the second expedition, Josephine bore Peary a daughter, Marie Ahnighito. The Eskimo people were intrigued by this white-skinned baby and delighted in calling her "Snow-Baby."

Peary returned home discouraged after the two-year journey; he had not traveled as far as he had hoped. But his enthusiasm soon rebounded when he was greeted as a hero. With renewed vigor, Peary set a goal for reaching the North Pole.

The Quest Begins

In 1898, Peary set off once more for Greenland. Setting up base in Ellesmere Island, Peary planned to cross the frozen sea to Fort Conger and then trek the remaining distance to the North Pole. But fierce winter weather and rapidly dwindling supplies forced him and his team to turn back more than once. At one point, Peary even had to have eight frostbitten toes amputated. Incredibly, he taught himself to walk again and within months Peary was ready to set off again. In all, this particular expedition lasted four years, and Peary set a record for reaching the most northern point to date.

Robert Edwin Peary. Image courtesy of Underwood Photo Archives/SuperStock.

To the North Pole

Peary determined that success lay in starting from a more northern point, but he needed a ship that could cut through ice more efficiently. With the help of the U.S. government, Peary and his fellow explorers, including Henson, set sail in July 1905 aboard the specially built *Roosevelt*. They landed at Cape Sheridan and began the trek to the North Pole. But severe weather struck again, and when the group encountered leads—the water between ice floes—too large to cross, they had to turn back. Closer than ever before, they had set another record for reaching the most northern point.

Success at Last

In 1908, Peary, now more than fifty years old, set off on the *Roosevelt* to Cape Sheridan as before, but he moved his supplies farther west to Cape Columbia. His supply team was able to get Peary to within 140 miles of the North Pole.

On April 2, 1909, Peary set off for the North Pole with Matthew Henson, four Eskimo companions, and forty sled dogs. Four days later, on April 6, 1909, Peary and his team reached the North Pole. He photographed Henson and the Eskimos, and they planted the U.S. flag.

Questions and Validation

On the trip home, Robert Peary was stunned to hear that explorer Frederick Cook had claimed to have reached the North Pole a year earlier. Debate swirled around the question of who had reached the Pole first, but after an audit of his records by the National Geographic Society, Peary was recognized as the true winner of the Pole race. In 1911, The U.S. Congress promoted Peary to rear admiral in acknowledgment of his accomplishments.

Robert Edwin Peary died at age sixty-three in 1920 and was buried in Arlington National Cemetery with full honors. For some, questions persist as to whether Peary's calculations may have been off; however, there is no doubt that Peary attained legendary status as an American explorer.

NAME: Robert Edwin Peary

BORN: May 6, 1856, Cresson, Pennsylvania

DIED: February 20, 1920, Washington, D.C.

MARRIED: Josephine Diebitsch

CHILDREN: Marie Ahnighito, Robert Edwin Jr.

ACCOMPLISHMENTS: On April 6, 1909, Peary, along with assistant Matthew Henson and four Eskimo companions, became the first person to reach the North Pole.

QUOTE: "The Pole at last. The prize of three centuries. . . . Mine at last! I cannot bring myself to realize it. It seems all so simple and commonplace."

Winter Laughter

Rebecca W. Thomas

From my warm fireside,
Steaming mug in hand,
I watch the children play
Knee-deep in fresh-fallen snow.
Their laughter echoes their delight
With snowmen and snowball fights.
They have rosy cheeks and soaked mittens
From making angels in the bank.
It gives me pause to reflect
On the child yet inside of me,
And revel in the innocence
And the pure joy of this day.

Winter's Song

Janet Goven

In the winter, days are shorter,
Air is frigid, trees are bare,
Gardens barren of their flowers,
Birds no longer singing there.

Grass is hidden under snowflakes,
Chimneys smoking, no surprise,
Diamond-studded sidewalks sparkling
Strolling under moonlit skies.

Lights are shining in each window
Games are played and books are read,
Fires are burning, hearts are yearning,
Hands are held while prayers are said.

Laughter ringing, songs we're singing
Time together, nights are long.
Families sharing, all declaring
Love is strong through winter's song.

*Artist Alexander Krazjewski captures the bliss
of a childhood Christmas in his original artwork
JOYFUL EVE. Image from Alexander Krajewski.*

Christmas Eve

Albert S. Reakes

Lanterns burn and bells are ringing.
To the woods the children go,
Picking evergreens and bringing
Holly boughs with mistletoe.
Twilight comes as day is ending,
Then around the Yule log fire,
Young and old, their voices blending,
Carol in a tuneful choir

To mankind the revelation
Of the light that came to earth,
Joining in the celebration
Of the Savior's lowly birth.
May the lone, the sad, the stranger
Joy and blessedness receive;
Come and worship at the manger—
This the call of Christmas Eve.

An open-hearth fireplace warms the dining room of a Colonial-style home. Photo by Jessie Walker.

Winter Nights

Mary F. Butts

Blow, wind, blow!
Drift the flying snow!
Send it twirling, whirling overhead!
There's a bedroom in a tree,
Where, snug as snug can be,
The squirrel nests in his cozy bed.

Shriek, wind, shriek!
Make the branches creak!
Battle with the boughs till break o' day!
In a snow cave warm and tight,
Through the icy winter night,
The rabbit sleeps the peaceful hours away.

Call, wind, call,
In entry and in hall,
Straight from off the mountain white and wild!
Soft purrs the cat
On her fluffy mat,
And beside her nestles close her furry child.

Scold, wind, scold,
So bitter and so bold!
Shake the windows with your tap, tap, tap!
With half-shut, dreamy eyes
The drowsy baby lies,
Cuddled close in his mother's lap.

A toddler plays peek-a-boo during a winter outing in artist Donald Zolan's original oil painting entitled Snowy Adventure. *Image courtesy of Pemberton & Oakes, Ltd.*

Caravan

Tammy C. Ferris

A caravan of Eskimos
trudged through the raging storm.
They fought the bitter winter winds
in the dawn of the early morn.

They climbed an endless pathway
one burdened step at a time,
while stiff, cold, aching fingers
clutched a rope of twine.

To the top of the lofty mountain
they tugged their treasured sleds.
Bright red "Western Flyer"
was painted upon their beds.

When they reached their destination,
they formed a wooden train—
a colorful parade of parkas
as down the hill they came!

The Child Inside

Sheila Gagen

What brings out
the child inside
more than a wintry day?
Snowflakes flitting,
drifting, shifting,
with not a one the same.
Forming caps for fence posts
with sleeves along the beams,
before it frosts the fir trees
to white confectioners' dreams.
Time for making snowmen
(those known men have three parts),
time for throwing snowballs
and trying to hit our mark!
Then we'll make our angels
that fly upon the ground.
We'll lie face up,
flap our wings,
and send them heaven-bound!
Hop up on your favorite sled;
go flashing through the scene.
Laugh until you lose your breath
among the blanketed evergreens.
What brings out
the child inside
more than a wintry day?
The snow is falling—
calling, calling,
"Come out! It's time to play!"

A young girl giggles with glee as she plays in the falling snow.
Photo by Bon Color Photo Agency/ImageState.

Christmas Memories

Deborah A. Bennett

I remember Christmases of long, long ago
And midnight windows all aglow,
Of green pine limbs, of candlelight,
And snowy moons like stringless kites.

I remember Christmases of long, long ago
And the sequined wind that whispered low
Of silvery ponds we longed to skate
And crystal hills that wait and wait.

I remember Christmases of long, long ago
And twinkling sleigh bells, as the white stars glow,
Of kitchens of prayers and pumpkin pies
And chestnuts warm, as the firelights rise.

Of holly and berries and mistletoed kisses,
Of ruby-ribboned boxes, of secret wishes,
Of bright, child voices ringing through the snow—
I remember Christmases of long, long ago.

Watercolor artist Diane Phalen depicts winter fun in the country in
WINTER CROSSING. *Image courtesy of Diane Phalen Watercolors.*

REMEMBER WHEN

Lillian Smith

WHEN PECANS STARTED FALLING
from *Memory of a Large Christmas*

Christmas began when pecans started falling. The early November rains loosened the nuts from their outer shells and sent them plopping like machine gun bullets on the roof of the veranda. In the night, you'd listen and know IT would soon be here.

IT was *not* Thanksgiving. . . . We eased over the national holiday without one tummy ache. Turkey? That was Christmas. Pumpkin pie? Not for us. Sweet potato pie was Deep South dessert in the fall. We had it once or twice a week. Now and then, Mother varied it with sweet potato pone—rather nice if you don't try it often: raw sweet potato was grated, mixed with cane syrup, milk, eggs, and spices and slowly baked, then served with thick unbeaten cream; plain, earthy, caloric and good. But not Christmasy.

Pecans were. Everybody in town had at least one tree. Some had a dozen. No matter. Pecans were prestige. They fit Christmas.

And so you lay there, listening to the drip-drip of rain and plop-plop of nuts, feeling something good is going to happen, something good and it won't be long now. And you'd better sneak out early in the morning before your five brothers and three sisters and get you a few pecans and hide them. Strange how those nuts made squirrels out of us. Nothing was more plentiful and yet we hid piles of them all over the place. Of course,

when there are nine of you and the cousins, you get in the habit of hiding things. . . .

But on tree-shaking day we were meek. We said proper verses, we bowed our heads for the blessing, we ate quickly, did not kick each other or yap at Big Grandma.

Thousands of nuts fell until sheets were covered and thickening.

The moment we were excused from the table we ran to the linen closet for old sheets and spread them under the trees as our father directed. We got the baskets without being told. We were gloriously good. . . .

Whoever won by fair or foul means the title of shaker of the tree did a pull-up to the first limb, hefted himself to the next, skittered into the branches and began to shake. Thousands of nuts fell until sheets were covered and thickening. Everybody was picking up and filling the baskets, except the little ones who ran round and round, holding their hands up to catch the raining nuts, yelping when hit, dashing to safety, rolling over the big boys' bird dogs, racing back. . . .

This was how Christmas began for us. Soon, the nuts had been stored in old pillow cases. Our neighbors used croker sacks; I don't know why we preferred old pillow cases. After a few days of what

Mother guards her Christmas cake from her little one. Photo from Retrofile.com.

the cold air to harden while watchers take turns shooing the hen away and bird dogs away and the cat. . . .

Christmas Eve came. All day, Mother and Grandma and the cook and the two oldest sisters worked in the kitchen. Fruit cakes had been made for a month, wrapped in clean white towels, and stored in the dark pantry. But the lean pork had to be ground for pork salad, the twenty-eight-pound turkey had to have its head chopped off, and then it must be picked and cleaned and hung high in the passageway between house and dining room, and then, of course, you had to put a turkey feather in your hair and make like you were Indians; then coconuts had to be grated for ambrosia and for the six-layered coconut cake and then eight coconut custard pies, and you helped punch out the eyes of the coconuts; then of course you needed to drink some of

our mother called "seasoning," the picking out of the nut meats took place. . . . But when Big Grandma was there, she shooed us away, ensconced herself in a rocker in a sunny place on the circular veranda, and, as she rocked and sang "Bringing in the Sheaves," she carefully cracked the nuts (she was good at it) and got them out whole; and she'd put three halves in the fruit jar and plop one in her mouth for the road, but finally quarts and quarts of pecan halves were ready for the fruit cake, and the date and pecan cake, and the Waldorf salad and the chicken salad and the chewy syrup candy you make from cane syrup with lots of homemade butter and lots of nuts—the kind you put on the back veranda for

the coconut milk, and, as you watched the grownups grate the nut meats into vast snowy mounds, you nibbled at the pieces too small to be grated—and by that time, you felt sort of dizzy but here came the dray from the depot bringing the barrel of oysters in the shell (they were shipped from Apalachicola), and you watched them cover the barrel with ice, for you can't count on north Florida's winter staying winter. It was time, then, to lick the pan where the filling for the Lord Baltimore cake had been beaten and somebody laid down the caramel pan—but you tried to lick it and couldn't, you felt too glazy-eyed and poked out. And finally, you lay down on the back porch in the warm sun and fell asleep.

DECEMBER

Henrietta Cordelia Ray

List! list! the sleigh bells peal across the snow;
The frost's sharp arrows touch the earth and lo!
How diamond-bright the stars do scintillate
When Night hath lit her lamps to Heaven's gate.
To the dim forest's cloistered arches go,
And seek the holly and the mistletoe;
For soon the bells of Christmastide will ring
To hail the Heavenly King!

A CHRISTMAS CALL

Henry Snyder Alleman

Come, Christmas, as before,
To all the world tonight;
Come, Christmas, as of yore,
With sweet and holy light.

Sing, angels, from above,
The holy song of old.
Sing, angels, of His love
In accents sweet and bold.

Hear, world, the song sublime
Of peace on earth, good will.
Hear, world, the voice divine;
In reverence be still.

Adore, people of the earth,
This Holy Child, the King,
Adore, people, before Him fall,
Your gifts of love to bring.

For there is born to you this day in the city of David a Savior, who is Christ the Lord.
~ Luke 2:11 ~

Artist Valorie Evers Wenk captures the stillness of this most holy night in her original painting entitled CHRISTMAS EVE.

READERS' REFLECTIONS

Readers are invited to submit original poetry for possible publication in future issues of IDEALS. *Please send typed copies only; manuscripts will not be returned. Writers receive payment for each published submission. Send material to Readers' Reflections, Ideals Publications, 535 Metroplex Drive, Suite 250, Nashville, Tennessee 37211.*

THE REAL CHRISTMAS

Helen Gregory
Florissant, Missouri

When I was just a little girl
Christmas was to me
Carols, lights, toys, delight,
Anticipation just to see
What lay beneath the tree for me.

Mounds of snow, sleighs and bells,
Christmas was to me
Stockings, candy, fireplaces,
Long weekends with friendly faces,
But most of all, my tree.

Green and red decorations,
An angel all aglow,
But I confess what I liked best
Were gifts that lay below.

I thought I knew the meaning
Of Christmas and His birth

But as a child my thoughts gave way
To trees and toys of worth.

But Christmas trees soon dry out
As presents are unwrapped;
What's left behind is hard to find,
Though riches are untapped.

If everyday were Christmas
And the love we share that day
Could be given to the lonely
To bring a golden ray,

Then the world could be a Christmas tree,
Shining near and far,
Bringing hope to all who need
A special Christmas star.

SENTIMENTAL CHRISTMAS

Bernice Roche Jacobs
Washington, Pennsylvania

There's a sentimental Christmas
In the corner of my heart;
The place I keep my treasures,
So we will never part.

It's filled with loving faces
And the voices I hold dear.
It's a sentimental journey,
And I take it every year.

First I stroll the busy sidewalk,
Where the happy snowflakes play;
Watch them kiss each amber streetlamp
That they pass along their way.

I greet the corner Santa,
Hear the distant church bells chime.
Then I'm filled with awe and wonder
At that old-time five and dime.

Now I push that old door open,
And magic fills the air.
There are paper bells and tinsel
And music everywhere.

I shop the candy counter,
I go down the wooden stair.

And no computers hum,
And no escalators are there.

Just aisles and aisles of treasures
As far as I can see;
And the bubble lights are dancing
On that old-time Christmas tree.

When at last my arms are laden
With gifts I've chosen with care,
I start that pathway homeward
Through the twilight's frosty air.

I can smell the scent of woodsmoke
Combined with fresh-cut pine;
And the candle lights from windows
On the holly berries shine.

And I know home's door will open;
Loving arms await me there.
And once more I'm a child again
Without a single care.

How I'll kiss those loving faces,
Hear sweet voices I recall.
It's my sentimental Christmas;
May God bless us one and all.

Christmas Pageant

Eileen Spinelli

The children
dressed in paper gowns,
crumpled halos,
clattering coat hanger wings
teach us so many
wise and tender things,
teach us most that we are
all of us angels
trembling against
poster-painted skies,
all of us
more beautiful,
more capable of peace
than we realize,
all of us starry
and full of zany song.
Come to the cardboard inn,
come with the children.
There is room now—
yes,
it is Christmas
and there is room.

*Children prepare for the Christmas pageant
in artist Meredith Johnson's original artwork
entitled* FOLLOW THAT STAR.

FAMILY RECIPES

PUMPKIN-PECAN BREAD

Sharon Goddard, Ben Wheeler, Texas

1	15-ounce can pumpkin	½	teaspoon ground cinnamon
½	cup cooking oil	½	teaspoon ground cloves
2½	cups all-purpose flour	1	teaspoon pumpkin pie spice
2	cups granulated sugar	½	cup chopped pecans
1½	teaspoons baking powder	½	cup semisweet chocolate chips
¼	teaspoon salt		(optional)
1½	teaspoons baking soda		

Preheat oven to 325° F. In a large mixing bowl, combine pumpkin and oil; set aside. In a separate large mixing bowl, stir together flour, sugar, baking powder, salt, baking soda, cinnamon, cloves, and pumpkin pie spice. Add dry mixture to pumpkin mixture and stir until blended. Stir in pecans and chocolate chips (if desired). Spoon batter into two greased 8½-by-4½-by-2½-inch loaf pans. Bake 1 hour and 15 minutes or until toothpick inserted in center comes out clean. Cool 10 minutes in pan on wire rack. Makes 2 loaves.

DATE-NUT BREAD

Phyllis M. Peters, Three Rivers, Michigan

1	cup apple juice, heated until hot	½	teaspoon nutmeg
1	cup chopped dates	1	teaspoon baking soda dissolved
1	cup brown sugar, packed		in 1 tablespoon warm water
2½	cups all-purpose flour	2	tablespoons butter
1	teaspoon baking powder	1	egg, beaten
1	teaspoon cinnamon	1	cup chopped walnuts

Preheat oven to 325° F. In a small bowl, combine hot apple juice and dates; set aside to cool. In a large mixing bowl, stir together with a fork the brown sugar, flour, baking powder, cinnamon, and nutmeg; set aside. In a separate large mixing bowl, stir together baking soda, butter, and egg. Add cooled dates and apple juice to egg mixture. Add dry mixture to egg mixture and stir until blended. Fold in walnuts. Spoon batter into two greased 8½-by-4½-by-2½-inch loaf pans. Bake 45 minutes or until toothpick inserted in center comes out clean. Cool 10 minutes in pan on wire rack. Makes 2 loaves.

ORANGE-GLAZED HOLIDAY BREAD

Jeanette Braden, Lafayette, Indiana

2 cups all-purpose flour
¾ cup granulated sugar
2 teaspoons baking powder
½ teaspoon salt
1 cup raisins
1 cup peeled and shredded apple
1 cup milk

2 tablespoons butter, melted
1 egg, beaten

Glaze:

¼ cup orange juice
2 tablespoons light corn syrup
⅓ cup powdered sugar

Preheat oven to 350° F. In a large mixing bowl, stir together flour, sugar, baking powder, and salt. Stir in raisins and shredded apple; set aside. In a separate large mixing bowl, combine milk, butter, and egg; whisk until well blended. Add dry ingredients to egg mixture and stir until blended. Pour batter into one greased 9-by-5-inch loaf pan. Bake 1 hour or until toothpick inserted in center comes out clean. Cool 10 minutes in pan on wire rack. In a small bowl, stir together orange juice, corn syrup, and powdered sugar until well blended. Insert holes in bread with skewer and pour glaze over bread. Makes 1 loaf.

CRANBERRY-ORANGE BREAD

P. S. Biel, Denver, Colorado

2 cups all-purpose flour
1 cup granulated sugar
1½ teaspoons baking powder
1 teaspoon salt
½ teaspoon baking soda
¾ cup orange juice

1 tablespoon orange zest
2 tablespoons shortening, melted
1 egg, beaten
1½ cups coarsely chopped cranberries
½ cup chopped nuts

Preheat oven to 350° F. In a large mixing bowl, stir together flour, sugar, baking powder, salt, and baking soda; set aside. In a separate large mixing bowl, whisk together orange juice, orange zest, shortening, and egg. Add dry ingredients to orange juice mixture and stir until well blended. Add cranberries and nuts; stir well. Spoon batter into greased 9-by-5-inch loaf pan. Bake 55 minutes or until toothpick inserted into center comes out clean. Makes 1 loaf.

From the recipes sent in by Ideals readers, we've gathered an assortment of quick breads that make great last-minute holiday gifts. We would love to try your favorite recipe too. Send a typed copy to Ideals Publications, 535 Metroplex Drive, Suite 250, Nashville, Tennessee 37211. Payment will be provided for each recipe published.

Toys of Memory

Hilda Butler Farr

When Christmas comes I always plan
There'll only be upon the tree
The tinsel and some colored lights
And think the family might agree.
But every year the plans are changed
And all I say is laughed away;
Out comes the box of ornaments
Belonging to another day.
The snowman, yellowed now with age—
How memories stir of him and her,
The boy and girl that now are grown;
I watch it all with eyes that blur.
The tiny Santa Claus we bought
So long ago I hardly know
Just when it was, but they were small
(Back then it seemed they'd never grow).
And there's the little doll on skates,
All dressed in blue and pretty too.
To others they mean not a thing
And yet to us how much they do.
But if they take me at my word,
Well then I guess I must confess
I'll hunt the ornaments myself
With all the speed that I possess.
Because in spite of all I say,
I know our tree would never be
Complete without these little toys,
The treasured toys of memory.

Beloved toys are displayed beneath a Christmas tree of simpler times. Photo by Jessie Walker.

THROUGH MY WINDOW

Pamela Kennedy

A VIEW FROM THE TOP

I am getting older, but I always feel young again at Christmas. When the family gathers and the children come to celebrate, I thrill again at the ring of carols, the laughter, and the shouts of joy. In the quiet of candlelight, I have seen my family grow and change; I have observed their joys and sorrows. And although they do not even know I watch, I have the memories of every one of their Christmases stored within my heart.

I was a gift that first Christmas, from the mother of the bride. She thought the newlyweds should begin their own Christmas traditions. She found me at a craft fair, created by a pair of arthritic hands, donated by a generous heart. Fashioned from yards of simple white cotton thread, I measure a mere twelve inches in height, but every year, placed atop the Christmas tree, I spread my wings over the little family I have come to love.

That first December, they purchased a tiny pine and set it on a table. There wasn't money for ornaments, so one evening they sat together on the floor, cut and pasted strips of colored paper together, then adorned the evergreen branches with chains fashioned from their love. Then they placed me atop their creation, spreading my starched skirt over the pungent needles. I was there when they sat in candlelight and held one another in the soft, flickering glow, enchanted as children by their first Christmas as husband and wife.

Packed away in layers of tissue each January first, I waited patiently for the year to pass. Then rejoiced when it was time once more for holiday music and scents to fill the air. Boxes and baskets of Christmas decorations were hauled from their hideaways. There were beaded garlands, lights, and crystal icicles, but after the first year I was always placed upon the tree first. Then from my

Each Christmas they found their way home to celebrate beneath their own tree, under my outspread wings and watchful eye.

vantage I watched as the decorating continued. Each year the wife bought something new to hang upon the tree, something representing a place they had visited or an experience shared. Once it was a delicate blown glass ball made from the ash of a volcano. Another year it was a dolphin carved from koa wood on a tropical island. A filigreed oval from the White House joined us one year and another time it was a whole herd of embroidered satin horses from Hong Kong. My family traveled, but each Christmas they found their way home to celebrate beneath their own tree, under my outspread wings and watchful eye.

For many years it was just the two of them, then one December there was a little boy. His eyes shone as he gently pushed the bright balls and sparkling lights with a chubby finger. His father lifted him up and the baby stretched out his hand and grabbed my wings. He giggled as I swayed on the treetop, pulled askew by his grasp. Righted and straightened once more, I watched that year as husband and wife became mother and father, lovingly introducing their little son to the magic of Christmas.

Another boy and then a girl joined the family circle and holiday rituals changed as the children added their special touches to family traditions. The lovely purchased ornaments now hung side by side with macaroni stars and walnut-shell mangers, clothespin reindeer, and snowmen made from cotton balls. I alone observed as one young son, thinking no one saw, secretly pinched and shook the packages. And I smiled down as the other little boy slept one evening, curled up under the fragrant boughs, pretending to be camping in the woods. Once I watched the little girl creep out at night to play pretend with all the satin horses, and then to carefully rearrange them along the lower branches within easy reach. And I will never forget that fearful night when the cat shattered a porcelain ballerina and almost tipped over the tree in an effort to catch a velvet mouse resting temptingly on a green bough. Despite a few perilous moments, I survived all of it, courageously standing vigil on the treetop.

The children are now grown and no longer live at home. But still, at Christmas, they gather around the tree. And even though my skirts are no longer stiff or purest white, and my wings and halo droop a bit, even though my face has been retouched and my bodice mended, I still am placed with pride upon the treetop. And when the music plays and the candlelight dances across the faces of my family, I am once more filled with joy. This is Christmas. This is the gathering of hearts around a hearth, sharing love and memories together.

Pamela Kennedy is a freelance writer of short stories, articles, essays, and children's books. Wife of a retired naval officer and mother of three children, she has made her home on both U.S. coasts and currently resides in Honolulu, Hawaii.

Original artwork by Meredith Johnson.

Prayer on Christmas Eve

Nancy Byrd Turner

O wondrous night of star and song,
O blessed Christmas night!
Lord, make me feel my whole life long
Its loveliness and light!
So all the years my heart shall thrill,
Remembering angels on a hill,
And one lone star shall bless me still
On every Christmas night!

The Glowing

June Masters Bacher

It isn't the tinsel
That causes the glow,
Or colored lights shining
On new-fallen snow,
Not cards with warm greetings—
Though lovely they are—
And, no, not the gleam of
A trembling star
That causes a Christmas
To bloom in the heart
And prepares the spirit
A new year to start.

It's what one is feeling
And then something more:
A Prince-of-Peace caring
That opens the door
To those who are weary,
Or hungry and cold.
It's sharing the story
That never grows old.
It's knowing and showing
Good will to all men
That starts hearts to glowing
With Christmas again.

The family Christmas tree waits for the children to discover the treasures placed under its branches. Photo by Jessie Walker.

HANDMADE HEIRLOOM

Melissa Lester

TREETOP ANGELS

When I was a child, I knew the holiday season was just around the corner when a nondescript cardboard box arrived in the mail. I'm sure our postal carrier had no idea what precious cargo lay inside. But with one glance at my grandmother's handwriting, I knew some treasure awaited discovery. My mother would open the package with great care. Inside, tucked under layers of tissue paper and enveloped in newspaper, were ornaments handmade by my grandmother for each member of the family. For me, there were always angels. Grandma began making angels for me shortly after my birth. They lined my bedroom shelves and kept watch over my childhood. Her angels were beloved treasures, and they were always my favorite ornaments on the tree.

Angels began appearing on the Christmas tree more than 150 years ago. Tabletop Christmas trees became popular in America soon after the English royals Queen Victoria and Prince Albert were shown in the *Illustrated London News* posing with their children before a decorated tree in 1846. Christmas trees immediately became fashionable throughout Britain, and the custom spread to East-Coast American society as well. Handmade decorations were popular additions to the tree, so making Christmas crafts occupied many hours of a proper young lady's time. Along with quilled snowflakes and pouches for secret gifts, a lady might have made beaded angels and angel-shaped cookies.

As Christmas tree decorations have become more sophisticated, angel ornaments and tree toppers have also evolved through the years. Many have been imported from Germany, a center for Christmas tree traditions. *Rauschgoldengels*, or "tingled angels," were created in Germany in the 1850s. These tree toppers were dressed in gilded tin. By the 1870s, German-made glass ornaments had become popular on English and American

---

Angels were said to be symbolic of God's messengers of purity, peace, and love.

---

trees. The glass angels were said to be symbolic of God's messengers of purity, peace, and love.

In the Victorian era, trees became bigger and grander than ever. Full-size trees replaced earlier tabletop versions and were covered with as many decorations as possible. With the death of Queen Victoria in 1901, trees became more understated until the Dickensian nostalgia of the 1930s. Trees became large and fanciful again during this era, with a beautiful golden-haired angel placed on top as the crowning touch.

Today, angels on the tree still remind us of the proclamation of Jesus' birth in Luke 2:10–12: "Fear not: for, behold, I bring you good tidings of great joy, which shall be to all people. For unto you is born this day in the city of David a Saviour, which is Christ the Lord. And this shall be a sign unto you; Ye shall find the babe wrapped in swaddling clothes, lying in a manger."

Elaborately dressed porcelain angels with feathery wings recall the Dickensian era, while more rustic clay and tin angels remind us of simpler times in colonial America. One style equally at home on any tree is the crocheted angel. Placed amid strings of popcorn, cranberries, and pine cones, a crocheted angel adds a country flavor. Nestled into a tree with silk ribbon and fanciful ornaments, it imparts quiet elegance.

A crocheted angel tree topper can be crafted by beginning and advanced crafters alike. Patterns abound that feature a variety of stitches, hook sizes, angel heights, and thread types. Angels can be crocheted with cotton thread in white or cream for a vintage, old-fashioned look or pearlized threads with metallic-edged wings for a more contemporary design. A bedspread-weighted cotton is often recommended.

Treetop angels can be stiffened with fabric stiffener, heavy starch, or a mixture of equal parts white glue and water. Most patterns recommend that only the angel's skirt, wings, and halo be stiffened, which can usually be accomplished with the help of rust-proof pins, waxed paper, and plastic bags (used as temporary stuffing until the stiffener dries). Cones wrapped in plastic or waxed paper can also be used to hold the angel's skirt in place until the stiffener dries. Cones can be constructed from paper plates or crafters may purchase foam cones at a craft supply store.

A few years after I married, my mother presented me with a plain-looking cardboard box. Inside, tucked under layers of tissue paper and

Crocheted angel treetopper courtesy of Crochet Fantasy *magazine.*

enveloped in newspaper, were Grandma's handmade angel ornaments. Now each finds a special place on my Christmas tree, along with other family ornaments that we have accumulated through the years. Together they guard the tree and remind us of what is important. And whether they are handmade angels from my grandmother or paper angels made by my preschool-age sons, angels can always remind us of God's love, declared in Luke 2:13–14: "And suddenly there was with the angel a multitude of the heavenly host praising God, and saying, 'Glory to God in the highest, and on earth peace, goodwill toward men.'"

Melissa Lester is a freelance writer living in Wetumpka, Alabama, with her husband and two sons. She contributes to a number of magazines and authored the book Giving for All It's Worth.

Picture

O. J. Robertson

Today the forest
glistens white,
silvered with snow
that came last night.
The paths are gone,
no rabbits stir;

the only sound's
a scarlet whir
of cardinal wings
lifting high
into the blue
of winter sky.

Preparation

Jaye Giammarino

Under a blanket of glistening white,
Muffle all the land this night.
Let the world in silence wait
And with joy anticipate
The holy birth, the gift of love,
The brightest star to shine above.
Vesper bells prepare to ring

And from the highest rafters swing,
Send a reverential chime
Through the air in perfect rhyme,
Peal a hymn of love on earth
on the day of Christ's rebirth.
Christmas spirit once again
Put love in the hearts of men.

A quiet peacefulness descends on the Sawtooth Mountains of Idaho. Photo by Dick Dietrich.

The Christmas Story
Virginia Blanck Moore

Such common things of everyday
like lowing cattle, fragrant hay,
stars flung across a velvet sky,
and shepherds watching night go by,

Such common things, and yet they hold
the greatest story ever told—
the story of a Savior's birth
and hope for all of peace on earth.

Counting Sheep
Grace Cornell Tall

Last night,
In line with a flock of sheep
That jumped a fence
To help me sleep,
I saw a wobbly Christmas lamb.
He got as far
As the padlocked gate,
But being too small
To make the leap,
He was pushed aside
And made to wait.
Now, it isn't fair
And it isn't right
For little lambs
To work at night,
So I pretended I fell asleep
And I halted the line
Of the leaping sheep,
And I didn't count another head
Till the Christmas lamb
Was safe in bed.

*Sheep snuggle together in a cozy stable in
Valorie Evers Wenk's original artwork entitled
ALL IS CALM. Image © 2003 Wenk/Applejack Licensing.*

The Shepherds

Luke 2:8–14

And there were in the same country shepherds abiding in the field, keeping watch over their flock by night. And, lo, the angel of the Lord came upon them, and the glory of the Lord shone round about them: and they were sore afraid.

And the angel said unto them, Fear not: for, behold, I bring you good tidings of great joy, which shall be to all people. For unto you is born this day in the city of David a Saviour, which is Christ the Lord. And this shall be a sign unto you; Ye shall find the babe wrapped in swaddling clothes, lying in a manger. And suddenly there was with the angel a multitude of the heavenly host praising God, and saying, Glory to God in the highest, and on earth peace, good will toward men.

The Birth

Luke 2:1–7

And it came to pass in those days, that there went out a decree from Caesar Augustus, that all the world should be taxed. (And this taxing was first made when Cyrenius was governor of Syria.) And all went to be taxed, every one into his own city.

And Joseph also went up from Galilee, out of the city of Nazareth, into Judaea, unto the city of David, which is called Bethlehem; (because he was of the house and lineage of David:) To be taxed with Mary his espoused wife, being great with child.

And so it was, that, while they were there, the days were accomplished that she should be delivered. And she brought forth her firstborn son, and wrapped him in swaddling clothes, and laid him in a manger; because there was no room for them in the inn.

The Adoration of the Shepherds

Luke 2:15–20

And it came to pass, as the angels were gone away from them into heaven, the shepherds said one to another, Let us now go even unto Bethlehem, and see this thing which is come to pass, which the Lord hath made known unto us.

And they came with haste, and found Mary, and Joseph, and the babe lying in a manger. And when they had seen it, they made known abroad the saying which was told them concerning this child. And all they that heard it wondered at those things which were told them by the shepherds. But Mary kept all these things, and pondered them in her heart.

And the shepherds returned, glorifying and praising God for all the things that they had heard and seen, as it was told unto them.

Shepherds gather in adoration in Artist Stewart Sherwood's original artwork entitled A Child Is Born. Image © 2003 Stewart Sherwood, courtesy of Lang Graphics, Ltd.

The Adoration

Matthew 2:1–2, 7–11

Now when Jesus was born in Bethlehem of Judaea in the days of Herod the king, behold, there came wise men from the east to Jerusalem, Saying, Where is he that is born King of the Jews? for we have seen his star in the east, and are come to worship him. . . .

Then Herod, when he had privily called the wise men, inquired of them diligently what time the star appeared. And he sent them to Bethlehem, and said, Go and search diligently for the young child; and when ye have found him, bring me word again, that I may come and worship him also.

When they had heard the king, they departed; and, lo, the star, which they saw in the east, went before them, till it came and stood over where the young child was. When they saw the star, they rejoiced with exceeding great joy.

And when they were come into the house, they saw the young child with Mary his mother, and fell down, and worshipped him: and when they had opened their treasures, they presented unto him gifts; gold, and frankincense, and myrrh.

The stable animals encircle baby Jesus in Artist Stewart Sherwood's original artwork entitled SAVIOR'S BIRTH. Image © 2003 Stewart Sherwood, courtesy of Lang Graphics, Ltd.

The Flight

Matthew 2:13–15

And when they were departed, behold, the angel of the Lord appeareth to Joseph in a dream, saying, Arise, and take the young child and his mother, and flee into Egypt, and be thou there until I bring thee word: for Herod will seek the young child to destroy him.

When he arose, he took the young child and his mother by night, and departed into Egypt: And was there until the death of Herod: that it might be fulfilled which was spoken of the Lord by the prophet, saying, Out of Egypt have I called my son.

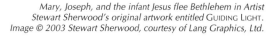

Mary, Joseph, and the infant Jesus flee Bethlehem in Artist
Stewart Sherwood's original artwork entitled GUIDING LIGHT.
Image © 2003 Stewart Sherwood, courtesy of Lang Graphics, Ltd.

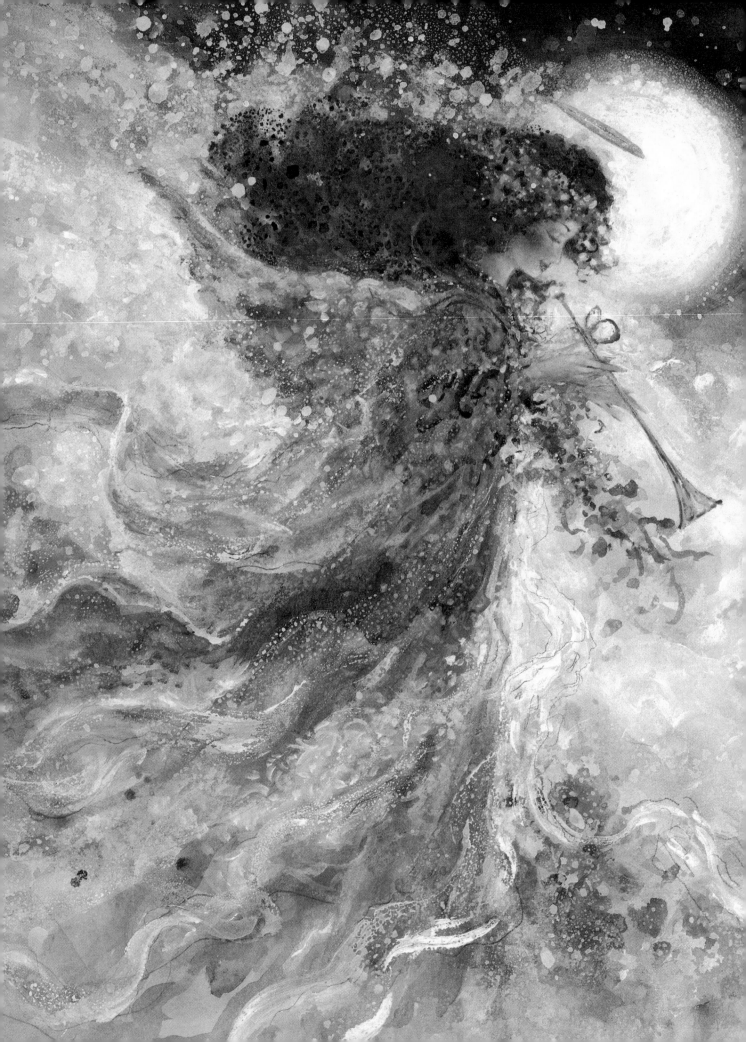

Christmas Chorus

Sara A. DuBose

When Jesus came down
His only crown
Was the jeweled-filled
Stars in the sky.
His throne was small
In the cattle stall,
His praise a lullaby.
And those who came
To give acclaim
Were men who
Smelled like sheep.
Yet shepherds heard
The angel's word
And now we all repeat:

"Glory to God
In the highest,
and on earth peace,
Good will toward men!"

For Christmas

Julia Collins Ardayne

Somewhere tonight a shepherd
His lonely watch is keeping,
And little towns, like Bethlehem,
Beneath the stars are sleeping.
And somewhere angel voices
Are caroling on high;
Across the world may stars of peace
Again shine in the sky!

This Is the Night

Ruth N. Ebberts

This is the night when folded hands
And quietness of heart,
Quite universally proclaim
What love and peace impart.

This is the night when heads are bowed
And there on bended knee,

The human soul experiences
A sweet humility.

This is the night when children sing
And chapel bells resound;
This is the night when prayer and faith
And Christmas peace abound.

On a Christmas Evening

Ruby Waters Erdelen

Dusk of evening glistens as it grays,
Unveiling bright new stars across the night.
Church bells chime, re-echoing their praise
To celebrate His birth. The mirrored light
Of windows' rainbow tint, a sparkling tree
Are glowing forms of love designed to bring
Joy in festive symbol. Melodically
We hear, "The First Noel," as carolers sing.
Beribboned gifts arrive from distant places.
Cards etched in color, sprigged with red and green,
Arrest my thought, bringing dear ones' faces
In fond illusion to memories' magic screen.
As I reflect, snow crystals frost the pane,
Bring glittering peace.
It's Christmastime again.

*The road remains passable to this meeting house in Sugar Hill,
New Hampshire, despite the snow. Photo by William H. Johnson.*

Trilogy
Lolita Pinney

Three Men were wise:
They traveled far
To worship an infant,
To follow a star.

Three gifts they gave
In stable stall:
Gold, myhrr, and incense
To King over all.

Three lives they led;
One light they saw.
Their wisdom lingers:
Love, joy and awe!

The Joyous Night
Mary B. Wilson

Tender the night,
Radiant the light
That shines o'er the stable bare.

Adoring the wise,
Loving the eyes
That gaze on the Child so fair.

Jubilant the song
Of the angel throng
That through the heavens rings.

Joyous the earth
At the humble birth
Of the promised Saviour and King!

"Adoration of the Magi" by fifteenth-century Italian painter Andrea Mantegna. Bridgeman Art Library, London/Superstock.

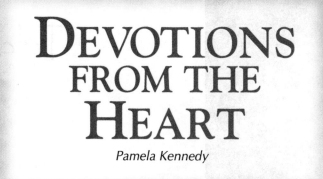

DEVOTIONS FROM THE HEART

Pamela Kennedy

But when the fullness of the time was come, God sent forth his Son....
—Galatians 4:4a

JESUS WOULD GO

Here in Hawaii there's a popular bumper sticker that states "Eddie Would Go." It refers to a courageous surfer, Eddie Aikau. Before the state of Hawaii had licensed lifeguards at Waimea Bay, an inlet notorious for huge waves, Eddie volunteered to swim out and rescue exhausted surfers and swimmers. Later, he became a certified lifeguard and, during his years of service, saved over one thousand individuals. Eddie never refused to take a risk for someone in need. In March of 1978, in heavy seas, he left his companions on a disabled Hawaiian outrigger canoe to swim miles across the open ocean for help. The damaged canoe was found by a rescue helicopter just hours after Eddie dove into the Pacific and all the passengers were saved. Eddie Aikau was never seen again. The bumper sticker celebrates the spirit of daring and sacrifice demonstrated by this modern Hawaiian hero. But the three short words also serve as a reminder to others to think about what a hero would do and then to do likewise.

It occurred to me as I was driving down the highway this December that at Christmas it might be appropriate for someone to hand out bumper stickers that say "Jesus Would Go."

When we had been foundering on the earth for millennia, exhausted by our despair and needs, Jesus left the comfort and glory of heaven to dive into our world on a rescue mission. Arriving in the small town of Bethlehem, Jesus lived His life in relative anonymity for three decades. Then the rescue mission began in earnest. He traveled from town to town, healing the sick, forgiving the sinful, releasing the captives. Wherever there

Dear God, thank You for coming to my rescue. This Christmas give me a heart of love and courage to reach out to others in need.

was need and despair, He went. Jesus ate dinners with tax collectors and hobnobbed with prostitutes. He taught children and grownups and even uppity lawyers and priests who thought they had nothing to learn. He performed miracles allowing the blind to see and the lame to walk and the deaf to hear. He fed thousands with a few bits of bread and a couple of fish, turned water into vintage wine, and told the sea to calm down. Regardless of how huge the waves of dissension and criticism, He rode through them.

And when it became apparent that the only way to rescue us forever would require the sacrifice of His own life, He went to the cross. He was lifted up and then put down, buried under tons of stone. It appeared for a few short days that He was lost, but then came the rushing tide of the resurrection pushing aside the rocks of disbelief and death, replacing them with hope and life. Then Jesus walked and talked with His disciples for forty days, along the banks of the very sea that once had threatened to drown them. He would be returning to the Father, He told them, but He would be sending the Spirit to live within their hearts for all eternity. And their assignment was to rescue others. The eternal lifesaving mission would continue.

At Christmas it is easy to focus on the simple beauty of the holy family at the manger in Bethlehem, but we lose so much if we remain beside the crib. The message of Christmas

A chapel welcomes a Christmas visitor in At Prayer by Bunol Laureano Barrau. Image from Christie's Images/SuperStock.

is more than angels and shepherds. It transcends carols and stars and candles. It is the affirmation ringing from heaven that the prophecies of the ancients and the predictions of the apostles are all true and that the fulfillment of God's Word will never be stopped. It is the understanding that each of us has the opportunity and obligation to dive into the world lapping at our doorstep and rescue those exhausted by their need and despair. Christmas is the heavenly echo of the everlasting promise: "Jesus would go."

Pamela Kennedy is a freelance writer of short stories, articles, essays, and children's books. Wife of a retired naval officer and mother of three children, she has made her home on both U.S. coasts and currently resides in Honolulu, Hawaii.

Remembered Christmas

Laura Baker Haynes

I once thought that Christmas meant sleigh bells and snows
And gifts gaily tied with bright ribbons and bows,
Till one day an old man with a much wiser head
(Who spoke not religion but lived it instead)
And knowing, on Christmas, the gifts would be few,
Succeeded in changing my whole point of view.
For pulling a chair alongside me one day,
He talked as he whittled an old board away.

"Christmas," he told me, "is a way of livin',
Not ours for the takin' but ours for the givin'.
The best gifts are not tied with ribbons and bows—
Things like love and faith and cheery 'hello's.'
And whether a Christmas is bounteous or lean,
It's the birthday of Christ—Do you get what I mean?"
The bell that he rang was as clear as could be,
And Christmas took on a new meaning for me.

Our snowman that year (best of them all)
Wore his stovepipe hat more stately and tall,
And the popcorn popped to the very last grain,
And somehow we managed one big candy cane.
The carols that year rang out so much sweeter;
Two little tin soldiers played follow the leader!
Though sparse were the gifts, the tree held much splendor,
For that year it glowed with thoughts of the sender!

Remembered Christmas! Could I ever forget
Those words of wisdom that abide with me yet?
Our Christmas that year was the best that we'd had,
For that wise old man, guess you know, was my dad.
Today, because of him, the snow falls whiter
And I know the star of the east shines brighter;
And whether a Christmas is bounteous or lean,
It's the birthday of Christ—Do you get what I mean?

Pink poinsettias and a vintage quilt speak of Christmases
spent amid the comforts of home. Photo by Nancy Matthews.

COLLECTOR'S CORNER

Laurie Hunter

VINTAGE ICE SKATES

My small collection of vintage ice skates decorates the foyer of my home at Christmastime and often sparks interest from my guests. These sporting accouterments of a bygone era lend a festive atmosphere to the entry hall and often inspire guests to imagine themselves gliding across a glass-smooth sheet of ice.

Not many of my holiday guests remember ice skating as an actual mode of winter transportation, but most like to daydream about it while inspecting the skates' worn blades and noticing the fine stitching. Many guests even check the skates' sizes to see if any pair might fit their own feet perfectly. When friends ask from where my collection came, I am sure they are expecting a romantic story of a childhood spent ice skating on country ponds. Really, they are simply a souvenir from my antique booth days.

I used to rent a little antique booth that I stocked with all sorts of finds I unearthed at estate sales and salvage stores. When I closed up shop, I decided to keep three pairs of skates I had purchased at a yard sale. When I found them, they were at the bottom of an old trunk full of moth-eaten coats and woolen mittens. They were just a dollar a pair, so I snatched them up and then researched their value. It turns out that the antique, clamp-on-style skates are more than one hundred years old and worth about one hundred dollars.

Thrilled, I polished the blades and the shoes, ironed the laces, displayed them in my antique booth, and began searching for more. Over the course of several years, I have assembled quite a collection of skates from countries such as Holland, England, Germany, and America. My favorite is a pair of "Sonja Henie Pleasure Skates," made by Nestor Johnson in 1938. The set, inspired by the famous Olympic great of the same name, includes skate guards, a pocket skate sharpener, and a signed picture—all in its original box!

What I love most about vintage ice skates is the romance that surrounds them. So many old movies, postcards, and paintings feature couples twirling around effortlessly, arms entwined, bodies leaning into each other on the curves, making perfect figure-eight grooves in the ice. In reality, ice skating can be a tricky sport; at least that has been my experience. But that does not deter me from envisioning myself gliding gracefully along, on one foot even, wearing one of the sets of magical ice skates from my collection.

COOL COLLECTIBLES

To begin a collection of vintage ice skates, the following information may be helpful.

HISTORY

• The invention of the ice skate derived from a need for improved winter transportation—a bone was attached to each foot with leather thongs and a staff was used to assist the skater in sliding across the ice.

• Modern skates were first developed in the 1300s by the Scandinavians, Finns, and Dutch, who strapped a metal runner to a shoe or a piece of wood.

• Ice skates were a standard mode of transportation in chilly climates from the 1600s until the early 1900s.

• Ice skating has been part of the Olympic Games since 1924.

• Theatrical ice-skating promotions, revues, and motion pictures during the twentieth century popularized skating throughout the world.

GETTING STARTED

• Some collectors choose skates made by one particular manufacturer, skates from a certain decade, or novelty skates featuring the signature of a famous skater.

• Collections can be limited to types of skates, such as metal skates, lace-up boot skates, or antique hockey skates.

• Other related items to collect include skaters' lanterns, skating trading cards, programs from ice skating shows, collectors' plates and figurines, vintage prints and posters, vintage skating attire, and even books about skating. *Hans Brinker* (also called *The Silver Skates*), for example, by Mary Mapes Dodge, one of the most famous children's books from the Netherlands, familiarized readers with the popularity of skating among the Dutch people.

TYPES OF SKATES

• Skates differ in blade types. A skate made for

Above: Handmade antique ice skates of American origin, c. 1840.
Opposite: Boot-top skates manufactured by the Barney and Berry Co., c. 1905.
Images courtesy of Russell Herner, author of Antique Ice Skates for the Collector.

racing features a light, all-metal blade. A rocker-shaped blade is used for figure skating. A short, thick blade is best for ice hockey.

• Children's skates were often double-bladed for stability as beginning skaters learned to balance.

WHAT TO LOOK FOR

• Consider the age of the skates, rarity, the manufacturer, the condition of the skates, and the patent design.

• Signatures from respected ice skate manufacturers add value.

• Ice skates that have seen decades of use can be highly collectible, especially if they are in good condition. Better still, vintage skates in mint condition, still in their original boxes, will fetch even higher prices.

WHERE TO FIND THEM

Look for vintage ice skates at antique shops, private estate sales, auctions, and antique shows. Collectors' clubs can be helpful and often feature their own newsletters. There is even a skating museum dedicated to the sport near Lake Placid, New York.

BITS & PIECES

$\mathcal{H}$e did not at all object to being the only man in the world,
so long as the world remained as unspeakably beautiful
as it was when he buckled on his skates and shot away into the solitude.

—*Elia W. Peattie*

$\mathcal{D}$own at the pond in zero weather,
To have a fine skate
The girls and boys gather.
Even the baby thinks it a treat
But somehow cannot stay upon his feet.

—*Nursery Rhyme*

$\mathcal{A}$ man learns to skate by staggering about
making a fool of himself; indeed, he progresses
in all things by making a fool of himself.

—*George Bernard Shaw*

$\mathcal{I}$t's a strange world of language in which
skating on thin ice can get you into hot water.

—*Franklin P. Jones*

$\mathcal{W}$e live amid surfaces,
and the true art of life
is to skate well on them.

—*Ralph Waldo Emerson*

$\mathcal{W}$alden is melting apace....How handsome
the great sweeping curves in the edge of the ice,
answering somewhat to those of the shore, but more regular!

—*Henry David Thoreau*

*T*he ice was here, the ice was there,
The ice was all around:
It cracked and growled, and roared and howled,
Like noises in a swound!

—*Samuel Taylor Coleridge*

*I*n skating over thin ice, our safety is in our speed.

—*Ralph Waldo Emerson*

*T*he sun makes ice melt;
kindness causes misunderstanding,
mistrust, and hostility to evaporate.

—*Albert Schweitzer*

*W*ait, Kate! You skate at such a rate
You leave behind your skating mate.
Your splendid speed won't you abate?
He's lagging far behind you, Kate.

—*David Daiches*

*T*rust not one night's ice.

—*Proverb*

SLICE OF LIFE

Edna Jaques

WINTER MORNING

A morning crisp as watered silk,
With blankets of new-fallen snow
Tucking the little houses in
For fear their naked feet will show;
The trees and shrubs are beautiful
Wrapped in their coats of carded wool.

The children on their way to school
In knitted caps and scarlet coats
Play hide-and-seek behind the drifts;
Their laughter rises high and floats
Above the highest maple trees
Like half-forgotten melodies.

The shop where mother buys the bread
Has glittering panes of frosted glass
Through which the lights take on a glow,
Like holy candles at a mass.
The streets are paved with softest down
As if a king had come to town.

A sleigh goes by with chiming bells,
Young people riding for a lark.
Their merry voices seem to ring
With extra sweetness in the dark,
As if they tasted suddenly
How lovely simple things can be

When Earth puts on her ermine wrap
And holds white diamonds in her lap.

Artist Robert Duncan was born in Utah and begin painting at age eleven, when his grandmother gave him his first set of oil paints. During summers spent on his grandparents' Wyoming ranch, he grew to love the rural life. Today, Robert, his wife, his six children, and a lively assortment of farm animals live in the little town of Midway, Utah.

Country-Boy Christmas

Tammy Crawford Ferris

I wish for you the Christmas joy
That comes to the heart of a country boy—
Carefree days of winter play,
Snowball fights and a ride in a sleigh,
Frolicking puppies and mischievous kittens,
A warm winter jacket and colorful mittens,
Peaceful cattle on a hill,
Snow-covered nights when stars stand still,
Peace in your heart from up above
Wrapped in God's Spirit and tied up with love.
My wish for you is Christmas joy—
The kind that's meant for a country boy.

Snowshoes rest in the corner of a cozy country cabin.
Photo by Nancy Matthews.

Chickadees

Minnie Klemme

Cheerful little chickadees,
How you stand the cold.
Ice and snow are all about,
Deep in winter's hold.

God has fashioned you with care,
Made of you a muff—
Feathers soft to keep you warm—
And it is enough.

The Winterbound

Lon Myruski

Spreading fields lie cloistered beneath
A fleece of fluffy snow
Where blue-cold hummocks loom confined
In crinkle-crankle rows,
And hoary trees steadfastly wait,
Trussed up in coats of rime—
Staunch captives held in custody
By winter's frigid clime.

Bespeckled trout peer longingly
Through icy crystal panes,
With dreams of leaping once again
Up from their lorn domain.
But gathered clouds of gray swirl forth
And gusting winds resound—
Another blizzard's 'bout to rage
Upon the winterbound.

An abandoned mine structure sheltered by aspens withstands a snowstorm in the Uncompahgre National Forest of Colorado. Photo by Dennis Frates.

From My Garden Journal

Laurie Hunter

HELLEBORES

As the children and I were walking through some natural garden paths near the Natchez Trace Parkway last winter, I decided to pause on a flat rock and take in a worm's-eye view. From the low vantage point, I spotted what I was looking for—hellebores, blooming right in the middle of winter. I was able to get in close to sketch the beautifully bold white blooms.

Inspired, I used my sketches to look up the variety at home. With a fitting common name of "Christmas rose," the blooms we had seen are called *Helleborus niger*. Pouring over the dozen or so species of hellebores that exist, I began sketching plans for adding some hellebores plants to my own garden.

Careful Cultivation

Hellebores thrive in the shade and particularly love the cool, chalky soil often found around the base of a garden wall or patio. So I planted our hellebores next to a wall near our new deck, adding some organic compost to help the area retain water and to increase the nutrient content of the soil. Another way to give hellebores the partial shade they need is to plant them along an informal woodland walkway. A year has passed, and now that the weather is frosty again, our hellebore plant is wearing pale blooms just above the level of the soil.

Classifying Hellebores

Hellebore is the common name of a genus of poisonous plants within the buttercup family. The European black hellebore, or *Helleborus niger*, features snowy white blooms and contains a powerful poison within its black roots; small amounts of this poison are sometimes used in medicine. The ancient Greeks believed that the hellebore could cure insanity; it was also reportedly used by the Greeks to poison the wells of enemies.

The false hellebore, white hellebore, and American hellebore comprise plants of an entirely different genus, *Veratrum*, of an entirely different family, the lily family. These plants are also poisonous and can also be used in medicine.

HELLEBORES

Caring for Hellebores

Although winter-flowering hellebores such as my *Helleborus niger* are frost-hardy, I baby them just a little. Since I enjoy cutting the blooms and taking some inside, where it's warmer to sketch, I've constructed a little mesh cloche to protect the flowers from mud splashes and inclement weather. A small pane of glass supported on either side by a few stones would work too. Taller species, such as *Helleborus argutifolius*, do not need special protection.

Although hellebores can be successfully grown in a wide variety of climates, the plants do not care for soggy soil, so it is a good idea to make sure the plants enjoy adequate drainage. Because mature trees soak up a great deal of moisture, planting hellebores near trees will ensure that the plants receive plenty of shade without having to endure waterlogged soil conditions.

Several varieties of hellebores make excellent container plants for the deck or patio, particularly *Helleborus lividus*, *Helleborus vesicarius*, *Helleborus x ballardiae*, *Helleborus x ericsmithi*, and *Helleborus x sternii*. These varieties have less extensive root systems than other strains of hellebores. They'll feel right at home within large, well-drained, terra-cotta pots filled with fresh organic compost.

One wonderful perk about growing hellebores is that the plants do not need to be dug up and divided every few years. Instead, once hellebores are quite at home in the garden, they will continue to bloom, year after year, without a lot of fuss and hassle.

All varieties of hellebores are long-living and strong; however, like most plants, they can be susceptible to diseases and pests. Mice, in particular, love to eat hellebore seedlings as well as buds and flowers from mature plants. Therefore, hellebores would always welcome an industrious cat to their garden home. Country gardeners in particular enjoy planting hellebores since their large green leaves are not the least bit appetizing to deer.

Early-blooming Beauty

Hellebores have always been one of my favorite flowering perennials because they bloom early and then look great for the majority of the year. They are also now available in a variety of stunning colors—from deep purple to sunny yellow and even a pale green, chartreuse, or coral color. Many gardeners prefer the Lenten rose, *Helleborus orientalis*. This variety boasts beautiful plants with evergreen leaves. Another favorite is the Corsican hellebore, or *Helleborus argutifolius*. Its whiskery leaves and pale green flowers beam all winter and into the spring, at which time its stems can be snipped off and new shoots will replace them.

My absolute favorite hellebore remains the Christmas rose, though, and now serves as the solid backbone in my garden. Even though my hellebore plants do not always bloom in time for Christmas, their velvety white blossoms arching up through the snow serve as a beautiful reminder of the Christmas spirit in my heart.

Laurie Hunter lives with her husband, Tim, and two children, Alexis and Oliver, in Leiper's Fork, Tennessee.

New Year's Eve
Grace V. Watkins

My father carried a lantern; still
I can see the path of the flickering light
On the snow and hear the crackling cold
Of the prairie night.

Still I can smell the fragrant warmth
In the little church and feel the glow
Of infinite peace that flooded my heart
Long ago.

The noise and the festive crowds grow dim
On a city thoroughfare,
And I kneel in a church on a wind-wide plain
In holy prayer.

The Star Still Shines
Eileen Spinelli

The star still shines
on our rooftops;
Angels still twirl
in the snow.
Joy still tempers
the winter chill,
just as it did long ago.
Love still seeps
through the lonely cracks;
longings for peace still ring true.
Christmas—
as old as a stable—
comes to make everything new.

*A Christmas sled waits for its next rider
to speed across the new-fallen snow.
Photo by Nancy Matthews.*

READERS' FORUM

Snapshots from our IDEALS readers

Above: Ashleigh Louden, age six, bundles up for a winter visit with her grandmother, Patricia Louden, in the snowy hills of Huntington, West Virginia.

Left: Amy Mulgrew of Tobaccoville, North Carolina, sent in this snapshot of her eight-month-old son, Matthew Alexander Mulgrew. Little Matthew is the grandson of *Ideals* subscribers Charlotte and Aaron Bullins.

Bottom: Venus E. Bardanouve of Harlem, Montana, says that her great-grandson, Aaron Kuntz, took his role in the Christmas play quite seriously and demonstrates the joy the shepherds felt when they saw the baby Jesus in the manger.

Top: Devoted family pet Harley poses for a picture with little brothers Henry and Sam, grandsons of Mary Estep of Fort Thomas, Kentucky.

Right: Proud grandmother Marcia Hancock of Shoreline, Washington, shares this holiday photo of three of her seven grandchildren, Douglas, Lauren, and William Hancock.

Bottom: Two-year-old Joseph Alexander Stoy takes a break from the Christmas festivities. Joseph is the son of Stanley and Angie Stoy of Charlotte, North Carolina, and grandson of Stanley J. and Betty Stoy of Nanticoke, Pennsylvania.

THANK YOU for sharing your family photographs with *Ideals.* We hope to hear from other readers who would like to share snapshots with the *Ideals* family. Please include a self-addressed, stamped envelope if you would like the photos returned. Keep your original photographs for safekeeping and send duplicate photos along with your name, address, and telephone number to:

Readers' Forum
Ideals Publications
535 Metroplex Drive, Suite 250
Nashville, Tennessee 37211

ideals

Publisher, Patricia A. Pingry
Associate Publisher, Peggy Schaefer
Editor, Lisa Carol Ragan
Designer, Marisa Calvin
Copy Editor, Melinda Rathjen
Editorial Assistant, Patsy Jay
Contributing Editors, Lansing Christman,
Pamela Kennedy, and Laurie Hunter

ACKNOWLEDGMENTS

ALLEMAN, HENRY S. "A Christmas Call." Used by permission of Josephine J. Lay. BACHER, JUNE M. "The Glowing." Used by permission of George W. Bacher. FARR, HILDA BUTLER. "Toys of Memory." Used by permission of Elsie Farr Day. JAQUES, EDNA. "Winter Morning" from *The Golden Road* by Edna Jaques. Published by Thomas Allen Ltd, 1953. Used by permission of Louise Bonnell. KLEMME, MINNIE. "Chickadees." Used by permission of Herbert L. Klemme. SMITH, LILLIAN. An excerpt from *Memory of a Large Christmas* by Lillian Smith. Copyright © 1962 and renewed 1990 by the author. Originally appeared in *Life* magazine in 1961. Used by permission of W. W. Norton & Co., Inc. TURNER, NANCY BYRD. "Prayer on Christmas Eve." Used by permission of Margaret Fleury Hutcheson, executor to the heir's estate. Our sincere thanks to the following heirs whom we were unable to locate: The estate of Agnes Davenport Bond for "The Homey Road"; The estate of Laura Baker Haynes for "Remembered Christmas"; The estate of Lolita Pinney for "Trilogy"; and the estate of Grace V. Watkins for "New Year's Eve."

Top: Six-week-old Nathan Thomas Lawrence dressed in his best attire for the Christmas Eve service at church. Little Nathan is the grandson of Connie Tromp of Rhinelander, Wisconsin, who still has an *Ideals* magazine from the 1950s that she's sure her grandson will one day enjoy.

Bottom: Nine-year-old Tommi Rae Hunter of Owego, New York, shows off her junior bridesmaid dress for the camera. Tommi Rae is the granddaughter of Robert and Juanita McMicken of Sparks, Nevada.